KONSHAUBI

A TRUE STORY
of PERSECUTED
CHRISTIANS
in the
SOVIET UNION

GEORGI
VINS

BAKER BOOK HOUSE
Grand Rapids, Michigan 49516

ISBN: 0-8010-9305-8

Printed in the United States of America

Contents

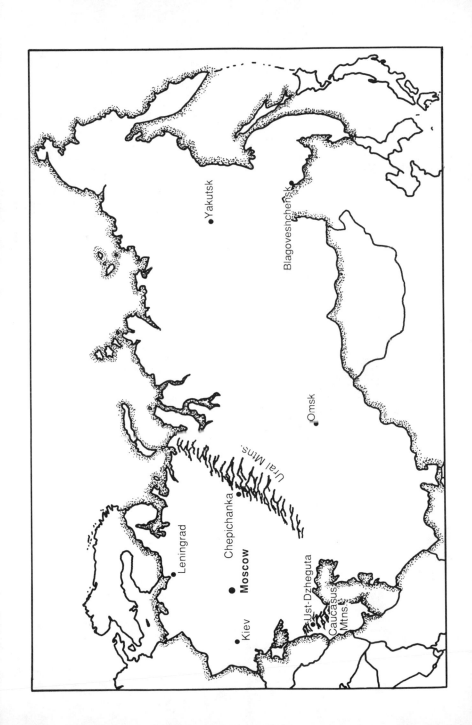

About the Author

This is a true story of Christians in a Soviet labor camp. Its author, Georgi Vins, is uniquely qualified to present this account. Soon after his birth in Blagoveschensk, Siberia, in 1928, Georgi Vins began learning about the persecution of Christians firsthand.

Georgi's father, Peter, was an American missionary who gave up U.S. citizenship, choosing to remain in Soviet Russia at a time when many people were fleeing. Peter was arrested three times for preaching the Gospel, and died in a Siberian labor camp in 1943.

Georgi was only seven when he saw his father for the last time. But the faithful example of his father and many other men of God who died as martyrs was to have a profound and lasting influence on his life. His mother, Lydia, made sure that Georgi understood the cost as well as the benefits of following Jesus Christ.

At the age of sixteen Georgi Vins was baptized in Omsk, Siberia. He started preaching when he was eighteen, and was also active in the choir and the youth

group of his church. When he graduated from the Kiev
Polytechnical Institute, he continued his ministry in
the church while working as an electrical engineer to
support his family. In 1962 he was ordained as an
evangelist of the Baptist church in Kiev by Alexander
Shalashov, a well-known Russian Baptist leader. In
1966 Georgi Vins was arrested in Moscow and sentenced to three years' imprisonment. He spent one year
in Lefortovo Prison and two years at camps in the Ural
Mountains. After his release he resumed his ministry.

In 1974 Georgi Vins was arrested again and sentenced to ten years' deprivation of freedom for his work
as General Secretary of the Council of Evangelical
Baptist Churches, the leadership body of two thousand
persecuted congregations. However, halfway through
his sentence he was suddenly transferred from a prison
in Siberia to a prison in Moscow. On April 27, 1979, he
was stripped of his Soviet citizenship and exiled to the
United States of America as one of five Soviet prisoners
of conscience exchanged for two captured Soviet spies.
The negotiations, transacted with the personal involve-
ment of heads of state Leonid Brezhnev and Jimmy
Carter, permitted Georgi Vins' family to join him in
America six weeks later.

Now Georgi Vins lives and works in Elkhart, Indiana, where he has opened an office dedicated to the task
of representing, defending, and aiding Christians in
the Soviet Union. He was forced to leave the persecuted
brethren in Russia, but his heart remains with them
and he speaks out on their behalf.

Thus, this book is not his story. It is theirs.

Foreword

Konshaubi

I first met Konshaubi Dzhange-tov in the spring of 1967 in a Soviet labor camp in the Ural Mountains. We were both serving our first terms of imprisonment for preaching the Gospel.

Circassian by birth, Konshaubi grew up in a Muslim village in the Caucasus Mountains in southern Russia. He was just a boy when he first heard of Jesus Christ, the "Russian God." Although Konshaubi was persecuted and rejected by his Muslim family when he told them of his new faith, it wasn't until he began to preach the Gospel to his people in their own language that the Soviet authorities took notice of his activities and arrested him.

In October 1985 Konshaubi began his third term of imprisonment for preaching the Gospel. As he continues to spend long years behind massive prison gates, my heart longs to encourage him, to ease the burden of his bonds, and to strengthen and comfort his family. It is my great desire that thousands of Christians around the world come to know and love Konshaubi, to remember him in his bonds, and to pray for him and his family.

Forty million Muslims live in the Soviet Union. Most of them have never heard the Gospel of Jesus Christ. Konshaubi, and others like him, who are explaining God's plan of salvation to their countrymen, desperately need our prayers. May the people which sit in darkness see a great light.

Georgi P. Vins

1

A Northern Transit

Spring came early in 1967—but not in the North.

In the North it was bitterly cold. There in the frozen forest of the Ural Mountains, three large trucks crammed with prisoners lurched from side to side, creaking and groaning, crawling over the snow-covered roads. All day long the trucks pressed onward, pushing ever farther and farther north.

Under the watchful eyes of soldiers with machine guns, we prisoners sat on the open beds of the trucks. On my truck about twenty of us were squeezed against one another so tightly that it was impossible to budge our swollen hands and feet. Every bump in the unpaved road, every sharp turn and pothole meant pain for us

13

prisoners. Our capped heads bobbed violently in time with the jolting of the vehicles. And thus we traveled the entire day without food or water.

Behind our backs, a metal screen divided off a section of each transport for the soldiers, a guard dog, and the miserable pile of bundles belonging to the prisoners. The soldiers, of course, were dressed in sheepskin coats, warm hats, and felt boots. While the penetrating cold numbed our motionless hands and feet, the convoy officer sat comfortably beside the driver in the cab of one of the vehicles.

In sharp contrast to our misery, the scenery along the road was exquisitely beautiful, a forest preserved by winter snow. Sunbeams, icily brilliant, stabbed down past the stately pines and tall Ural cedars. The glittering white blanket shimmered with an iridescent blue. Fluffy clumps of snow clung delicately to the branches of the trees. Everything was clean, white, and perfectly still, like some fairy-tale kingdom. The dissonant roar of convoy engines rumbled rudely through the tranquil air.

The beauty and majesty of God's creation is truly amazing! What invigorating, fragrant air! The pure heavens—what a boundless, distant blue! It was wonderful to be moved overnight from the dark, dirty, stinking prison to the open, snow-clean forest. Even being in the heavily guarded transport, crowded like assorted baggage, could not lessen my exhilaration at the glory of our surroundings.

In the snow along the road, numerous footprints, both large and small, were clearly visible: signs of birds and animals in freedom. The animals had run riotously wherever they wished beside the road and deep into the forest—forward, back, leaping all about. No one ordered them how to live, where to run, or what to do. As for the birds—what can be said? They flew wherever they wished, leaving not a trace of their flight! Freedom! Liberty! How splendid it is!

But for me, a prisoner, all of that had been taken away. Now I was a slave, my life under the control of the convoy guards. My lot was to sit motionless under the sharp eyes of the soldiers, under the threatening muzzles of their automatic rifles and the fierce glare of the guard dog.

Of course, a frozen, hungry prisoner, whose hands and feet are numb, could not remain enthralled by the beauty of the forest for long. After a while, all he wants is to quickly reach a human habitation—warmth—even if it is a labor camp. Already the unknown camp toward which we steadily traveled deeper and deeper into the North was a welcome destination. We longed to get there—soon!

I looked at the prisoner sitting beside me on my left. He was skinny and unshaven, his face covered with thick red stubble. On his head he wore a thin, gray prison cap, not warm at all. His shapeless prison jacket was the same dull color. He looked just like a scarecrow. I knew that I looked the same. He and I had already become acquainted. His name was Vasily. He was my age, in his late thirties, from Moscow, and had been sentenced for fighting on a subway. We had been together in the same prison cell and had talked a lot about many things.

As we bumped along the road, Vasily stared at the sides of the transport truck. In the cold wind, his eyes were watering, and little tears fell into the stubble on his cheeks, where they froze. I felt so sorry for him. I wanted to encourage him somehow, to stir him and inspire him.

"Vasily," I said, "just look around us at this winter forest. What beauty! And to think that all of this was created by God!"

Vasily turned toward me in disgust. "Look at yourself," he said. "Do you know what you look like? You're all huddled up with cold; you're hungry, and still you say, 'Look at the forest! How beautiful!' Don't you see we're freezing? And all you talk about is God!"

It was true; I was cold, as were all the other prisoners in the truck. But my heart was filled with such joy and light. I even seemed to feel a little warmer as I thought of God. I knew who had created this amazingly beautiful winter forest. I knew who had created me, who had created all of us. I knew that God loves us, is ever mindful of us, and offers salvation and eternal life to all men!

As I told Vasily about these things, the other prisoners listened. Then the man on my right said, "You Baptists are strange. For you everything is God. They put you in prisons and camps and freeze you on these forest roads, and all you do is talk about God and try to make others believe."

It was still light when the convoy finally jerked to a stop in front of the first of three wooden fences surrounding the labor camp. Each fence was twenty-five feet high and topped with several rows of barbed wire. Large rolls of barbed wire lay in the space between the fences. Tall, metal gates in each fence provided the only access. Soldiers stood guard in watchtowers at every corner. At the harsh command of the officers, we tumbled out of the transports, our numb limbs clumsily attempting to obey. Immediately, right there on the snow, each of us was thoroughly searched. It is bitterly cold standing in your socks while soldiers and officers meticulously and systematically search your footwear. Farther off and all around, still more soldiers stood with automatics and large, German shepherd guard dogs.

At last, all of the prisoners, except me, were ordered to enter the labor camp. I was taken to the camp warden's office. Silently he began scrutinizing all of my papers: the Statement of Accusation, the Verdict of the Moscow Court, and other records pertaining to my trial. In all, there were close to one hundred fifty pages, which I carried in a large folder. Then he picked up my most precious possession—my Bible! I held my breath as the warden glanced through the pages of God's Holy Word.

"The Bible is a forbidden book!" he announced. "I will not allow it into the camp."

"How can it be that the Bible is officially forbidden in the USSR?" I protested. "The constitution does not forbid the Bible."

The warden sneered.

"There are written and there are unwritten laws," he said slowly. "We live by unwritten laws. This is the 'underscoring' of communistic and materialistic thought: the Bible is a harmful book, and as such it is forbidden. The written laws—the constitution and the like—these are not for you Baptists but for foreigners. Let them read our constitution." He laughed hoarsely. "Let them study it and see what great freedoms we have!"

It was obvious that the warden of this camp, isolated

as it was deep in the northern Urals, was an educated, sophisticated person. He understood well the intricate politics of the Communist Party and the government's two-sided public and private stands on religion and the Soviet constitution.

"How long is your sentence?" asked the warden, still flipping pages.

"Three years," I replied.

"Where was your trial?"

"In Moscow."

"That is all," he said abruptly. "Now you will go to your section. I will check your papers and return them. But I will not return the Bible!"

Then something amazing happened. Calling out the door to a prisoner who was washing the wooden floor of the corridor, the warden shouted, "Makhovitsky!" When the prisoner appeared, I literally trembled with sudden joy. It was Fyodor Makhovitsky, pastor of the Leningrad unregistered church, who had been arrested and sentenced to two years' labor camp. We embraced, joyfully greeting one another. Fyodor whispered quickly that he had been in this camp for two months.

Why had the warden suddenly summoned Fyodor? Why had he let us greet each other so openly and warmly in front of him, knowing full well that Fyodor was a believer too? Perhaps the warden was curious to see how we would respond to one another. He did not explain. He simply called for a guard and, after another search, I was admitted into the prisoners' zone.

2

Konshaubi

As soon as I got to the prisoners' zone I was surrounded by a group of convicts. I later realized that this is the custom. Newly arrived convicts—new "transits" as they are called—are always besieged by the "local" prisoners who want every scrap of news. All kinds of questions were fired at me: *Where are you from? What's going on in the world? How's life out there?* I sensed keenly the total isolation and separation from life in liberty under which they lived in this *taiga** labor camp.

One tall, thin prisoner told me, "I've been in labor

---

*The subarctic forest mostly of spruce and firs.

camps since I was sixteen years old. I'm twenty-nine
now. I can't even imagine what life out there is like!"

Five or six of the convicts led me apart from the rest.
They were clearly younger than I, in their twenties.

"Do you have any smokes? Tea? Money?"

The questions came quickly, insistently, accompan-
ied by sharp, demanding glances. This was my first
time in a labor camp and I was still not familiar with its
"rules."

"I don't smoke; I'm a believer—a Christian! I don't
have any money either. How is it possible to have
money in a labor camp?" I asked naively.

"Come on! Where did you sew in your money?" pres-
sured one of the convicts, jerking hard at my black
prisoner's jacket.

"We'll find it and take it anyway!" warned another.

I stood silently. How strange it all was that when I
longed only for rest and warmth after the cold, difficult
journey, I should now fall into the hands of these camp
robbers.

Off to the side I noticed a large, heavily built man
studying me intently. From his clothing, it was obvious
that he, too, was a prisoner. Now even more distracted,
I tried to end this strange and frightening predicament.

"Listen, fellows," I turned again to the convicts. "Just
tell me how to get to my barracks. I don't have any tea,
money, or cigarettes! I'm a Christian and was sentenced by a Moscow court to three years because of my
faith in God."

Muttering discontentedly, the group dispersed. Only
the one who had stood apart remained behind, watch-
ing, waiting. Wordlessly he began to approach me. I

eyed him warily. Large and powerfully built, his swarthy complexion, hooked nose, and huge black eyes made him appear even more threatening.

What does he want from me? I wondered. *Who is he? Why did he wait all this time until I was alone? Perhaps he is even more dangerous than the others who demanded money from me!* I turned away sharply and took a quick step toward the nearest barracks.

Suddenly he spoke. "Are you a brother?"

I stopped and stared at the approaching man. All at once his face was transformed by a wide, kind, almost childlike smile. It was, as our saying goes, "A smile that lights the soul!"

Could I have heard correctly? Who would speak such words here and in such urgent tones? And what a smile! Could this man be a friend—my brother in Christ?

Quickly I replied, "Yes, I'm a believer. What about you?" I extended my hand.

As he grasped it in a warm handclasp he said, "I'm also a believer—I'm your brother in Christ!"

We embraced, our eyes brimming with tears, and quick introductions followed.

My newfound brother in the Lord said, "My family name is Dzhangetov, and I'm called Konshaubi. I'm a Circassian, and my home is in the Caucasus. I used to be a Muslim, but at nineteen I believed in Jesus Christ as my personal Savior. For over twenty years I've followed him, and now I'm in prison for preaching the gospel."

Finding another Christian in the harsh surroundings of a desolate labor camp gave me joy beyond words. How difficult it is to be in bonds! But if there are two or

three believers imprisoned together—*that* makes a
church! A very small one, perhaps, but still God's precious church!

There were now three believers in our camp. We
could whisper encouragement to one another from the
Word of God written in our hearts.

3

Konshaubi's Story

So you used to be a Muslim but now you're a Christian. That's very interesting. Tell me more about yourself, Konshaubi," I asked on our first free evening after work. His face beamed as he started to tell me about his lovely mountain home and his people in the southern part of the Soviet Union.

In the mountains and valleys of the Caucasus, he said, live Circassians, a fiercely freedom-loving people. Even today, their total population is not over one hundred thousand. Theirs is a land where dazzling, snow-white peaks give birth to narrow, tumultuous mountain streams. In spring the valleys turn a rich emerald green before bursting into fragrant rainbows of wildflowers beneath a fathomless blue heaven, bright with the southern sun. The brilliant sunsets fade into an inky-black sky, bejeweled with glittering stars.

"That is my native land!" Konshaubi smiled proudly. "And my people are there, whom I love very much and who need Christ so much!"

Konshaubi went on to describe his childhood years. I could easily picture him, a little twelve-year-old shepherd, the youngest of his large family. Every morning he herded his family's small flock of sheep from the village and into a lush green valley. Konshaubi's parents died young, and he lived with his oldest sister and her family. Like most Circassians, they are Muslims. Konshaubi loved and respected his sister, who took the place of his mother and father. He also dearly loved his quiet, obedient sheep.

Not far from his home was a Russian village. Konshaubi often heard his family and neighbors speak about the Russians, of their life, their customs and their God. The elderly Circassian men told of the time, about a hundred years ago, when there was a great war between the Russians and the Circassians; but today they live in peace—a Russian town next to the Circassian village. Many of the Russians understand the Circassian language, and many Circassians (especially young people) speak Russian well.

In the center of the Circassian village was a beautiful mosque with a large crescent on top; in the center of the Russian town stood a beautiful church with a large cross. The Russians have their own God whom they call "Christ," Konshaubi was told, and they call themselves "Christians."

One day, some new officials went to the Circassian

village. They summoned the people for an important meeting in the square, directly in front of the mosque. There the officials made long, passionate speeches, shouting loudly and waving their hands energetically. Their main concern seemed to be the Circassian Allah and the Russian God "Christ." Over and over the officials repeated, "There is no God and there is no Allah!" After the meeting, they closed the mosque and hung a large lock on the door. Later the *mullah* (as they call the Muslim teacher) was taken to prison.

Gray-bearded old Circassian men shook their heads disconsolately and whispered among themselves. Before long the church in the Russian town was closed and locked too. The Orthodox priest was also taken away to prison. Within a year, both the mosque and the church became storage places for grain.

Young Konshaubi liked to ponder a great many things as he pastured the sheep all alone for days. Sometimes he thought about the Russian God. *Who is he?* he wondered.

One day when he was about fifteen years old, Konshaubi met a little old Russian man in the valley where he pastured his sheep. The man seemed very friendly and talkative. Konshaubi politely greeted the man who sat down beside him on a rock. A gentle breeze rippled the rich grass as the sheep grazed peacefully. A nearby spring of cold mountain water added its cheerful music to the whispered sounds of summer. The valley was quiet and tranquil.

"What abundance we have from God!" the man exclaimed as he surveyed the placid scene. "How lovely this spot of yours is!" Turning to Konshaubi he added,

"It's almost like it was for King David when he was a shepherd. Did you ever hear of King David?"

"No," replied Konshaubi. "Who was he? A Russian?"

"No, he was a Jew. The Bible tells about him. As a boy, he was a little shepherd looking after his father's sheep just like you. David loved God very much. Later he became king of all the nation of Israel. David wrote many songs, and the very best one is called 'The Shepherd's Psalm.'"

Konshaubi listened intently as the elderly man slowly recited the Twenty-third Psalm. Then pointing to the sheep the man said, "You are a shepherd of sheep, but the Lord God is the Shepherd of people. He loves you! He wants to be your Shepherd, too."

And that is how Konshaubi became acquainted with the Russian believers who called themselves "Evangelical Christian Baptists." Soon he began attending the believers' prayer meetings in the neighboring Russian town. There he met Christian young people and was given a New Testament.

But Konshaubi began to face growing hostility from his relatives. His oldest sister shouted at him, "You don't need the Russian God! Your god is Allah and Mohammed is his prophet, not Christ! Don't you dare go to the Russian meetings anymore!"

"It must have been very difficult for you," I sympathized.

"Yes, it was very difficult!" he replied. His face clouded. "My relatives became so angry at me for going to the meetings of the believers that they beat me several times. But I grew to love Jesus and his New Testament. When I was nineteen, I gave my heart to

Jesus Christ and was baptized. After that, I was forced to leave my home village."

Soon Konshaubi was married to a Russian girl called Tonya. She was a sincere, dedicated Christian. They settled in the city of Ust-Dzheguta, about sixty miles from Konshaubi's native village.

"Was there a church in Ust-Dzheguta?" I asked.

"Yes. We used to gather for worship services in an ordinary home in the forties after the war. About a hundred attended, including many young people and children. Once a week our teenagers conducted youth meetings. We had lots of singing and enthusiastic preaching. Often we visited neighboring areas and saw many repent and get saved. Then the authorities demanded that the church register, so we did. But after we registered, the authorities gradually put a stop to many of our activities. Young people were forbidden to gather for Bible studies and evangelize villages. Children weren't allowed to attend worship services. The leaders stopped baptizing people under thirty years of age."

"How did all of this affect your church?" I wondered.

Konshaubi sighed. "By the end of 1965 our group had dwindled to fifty people, and they were mainly older people. The AUCECB* senior pastor for the Caucasus area regularly visited our church, instructing us, 'Don't bring your children to the meetings! Don't draw young people to church! If you do, the authorities will take away your registration and close the prayer house!'

---

*All Union Council of Evangelical Christian Baptists, the group of registered churches whose leaders compromised biblical principles in order to win favor and recognition from the government.

"At first we were very submissive to these orders. We thought we could not survive without registration."

"Unfortunately, many believers thought that way until recently," I said sadly. "In the Ukraine where I lived, the senior pastors of the AUCECB tried to keep our children out of church, too. And then authorities went even further and told us, 'Don't tell your children about God. Don't pray in front of the children. Don't read the Bible to them. Otherwise, we'll take your children away from you and you'll lose your parental rights!' Well, you certainly understand what this 'registration' leads to and how atheism uses it to fight the church."

Konshaubi nodded and went on. "During the fifteen years we lived under registration, our church lost its children and youth. My wife and I have six children, and we saw our three oldest sons slip away into the world. Today, we agonize over the lost years, when we should have been teaching our children about God and taking them to gospel services anyway. Years later, we heard that many believers sacrificially stepped out in defense of the gospel, and that all across the country churches were springing up without registration. A group from our church became very interested."

"Konshaubi," I interrupted, "that's when a spiritual revival began! Praise the Lord that he revived you and me and called us to serve him! But how did you personally become part of the work of the revived church?"

His open, childlike smile was so incongruous with our surroundings. Konshaubi told me about the large meeting of the brethren in the Caucasus early in 1966. Those who organized it were elders and preachers from both registered and unregistered churches of the Caucasus. All had one thing in common: they were deeply burdened over the spiritual poverty in their churches. Of course, this conference had to be conducted secretly, without the knowledge of any government agencies or senior leaders of the AUCECB.

"I was invited to this conference," recounted Konshaubi. "For the first time I met a group of men who were dedicated to begin ministering according to New Testament principles. They took as their model the suffering but victorious early church. I was deeply moved by their willingness to sacrifice their freedom, even their lives, for the gospel and for spiritual renewal in our land. Some spoke of their burden for children, others of work among youth. The principle of complete independence from atheistic authorities in matters relating to spiritual service was upheld. Many workers gave short, ardent speeches, challenging us to join together in the revival which the Lord had begun in our country.

"This conference was held in a private home and for only one night; nearly one hundred and fifty men were present. We half-expected the KGB to discover us at any moment and arrest us. Yet we were so inspired by God's presence that we were ready for anything for the sake of Christ. After the conference I was convinced that it was absolutely imperative to do something in our church in Ust-Dzheguta."

Konshaubi paused, his dark eyes searching me earnestly.

"When I returned home," he went on, "I brought these matters before our church. First, the impossibility of continuing to serve two masters, and second, the danger of retreating further and further from the commands of the New Testament regarding baptism, the Christian upbringing of our children, and other fundamental issues."

Konshaubi leaned forward, speaking quietly. "I said very directly that we were guilty before God and must repent because we didn't allow children into the church and had refused to baptize our young people. Several members supported me, but the elder disagreed. 'You are a candidate for prison!' he warned. Within a week the senior AUCECB leader for our area arrived, and about twenty of us were expelled from the church. But this freed us from the fear of losing our registration and gave us the determination to start independent meetings in homes. Of the twenty people, five wavered, giving in to the fear of persecution. But the rest of us began serving the Lord on New Testament terms. Soon young people came to join us—the very ones who were kept out of the registered churches! Our children also began attending the services. Within two or three months there were fifty of us! We had no pastor, yet we met regularly three times a week in private homes. Once a month an ordained minister from the nearest town visited us for baptisms and observance of the Lord's Supper. That's how we became part of the renewed brotherhood."

Konshaubi paused with a faraway look in his eyes. Then he went on.

"Six months after we left the registered church, I was arrested. I was tried together with six other men from the unregistered churches in the Caucasus. The court sentenced me to three years' imprisonment for my role in the life of the unregistered church of Ust-Dzheguta."

"Freedom of worship for six months, then prison! Are you depressed about this?" I asked.

Konshaubi thought a moment. "No," he answered deliberately, "this is the only right way. We must stand firm in our obedience to Jesus Christ and Bible truth!"

Only later did I learn just how much Konshaubi had suffered both in prison and while being transported to labor camp. He was a southerner, torn from the temperate climate of his homeland and shackled to the ice. He longed for his wife and children, wondering how they were and what was happening to them.

He told me about how the warden treated him when he got to the camp.

"I can't figure you out, Konshaubi. How can you, a Circassian—a Muslim—suddenly become a Baptist? Why do you want a Russian God?" he sneered. "See where he brought you? Into a land of ice, to this labor camp! Just remember, out in the forest the bear is the boss; but here, I am the only boss! Forget your Jesus Christ! There's only one true religion—communism—and only one god—Lenin! In Stalin's time, I used to shoot people like you!"

4

"Warped"

Warped was the nickname that prisoners had given long ago to the warden of Chepichanka, and it stuck with him. His surname was really Stannitsky, but "Warped" fit him better.

Life had indeed warped Stannitsky, bending him capriciously this way and that for nearly sixty years, but never breaking him completely. Physically, too, he appeared warped, as his spine was beginning to stoop slightly. Yet despite his stoop, he was still tall. With his short, metal-gray hair and blue-tinged, smooth-shaven jaw, he looked the cold, unpitying man that he was. Impersonal in manner, Warped was extremely severe with both officers and prisoners. When he spoke, his heavy-lidded gray eyes stared straight ahead. He was not a talkative man, at least not when he was sober. It was then that his vile temper was feared the most, and prisoners and officers alike scrambled to escape his notice. On the other hand, when he had been drinking, his tongue could be loosened considerably; sometimes he even joked, cursing often and vigorously.

When I arrived at Chepichanka, Stannitsky was a captain. For ten years he had been in charge of this half-starved logging prison camp, buried deep in an eerie maze of dense Siberian forests, murky swamps, and meandering rivers. In this harsh region, the winters are terrible with the temperature sometimes plummeting to -64 °F. You can hardly breathe; one gulp of this icy air produces sharp pains in your lungs. In summer hordes of mosquitoes and small gnats blacken the sky like clouds. In the forest, in the barracks, or even in the officers' lodgings, no relief from them could be found.

Before Chepichanka, Stannitsky had been a KGB colonel living in relative luxury in Leningrad. Brilliant, well groomed, and disciplined, he never dreamed that fickle political winds might one day shift their course and drive him to the desolate northern *taiga*.

After Stalin's death in 1953, the KGB had undergone an internal purge. Then KGB chief Beria and his closest associate were executed along with a number of their colleagues. Others were simply expelled from the KGB.

Although he soon fell into the bad graces of the new regime, Stannitsky fared better than most. He was demoted to junior lieutenant for the Ministry of

Internal Affairs and assigned as warden to a labor camp. Even this appointment came only through the "benevolence" of a KGB general who had been friendly to Stannitsky in his youth. He had to forget his beautiful Leningrad, the splendid Nevsky Boulevard, and the famous "white nights." Gone was his large salary, gone the blue epaulettes of a KGB colonel. Stannitsky and his family were forced out of their comfortable State-owned apartment. His wife divorced him, unwilling to exchange Leningrad for the fierce frosts and mosquito-ridden swamps of Siberia. Even his children renounced him.

After reaching the North, the former KGB colonel married a much younger woman. They lived in a small village near Chepichanka, but he found little happiness at home. Because his young wife was often distracted by the many young soldiers in the camp, Warped found himself in a constant state of jealous turmoil. His wife attempted to leave him several times, but each time he found her and dragged her home.

Still, within a few years, Stannitsky had risen in rank to captain, and by midsummer of 1967 he had become a major. Perhaps he could have risen even higher if he had stopped drinking vodka, which left him almost continually semidrunk.

In the settlement where the Stannitskys lived was a small store selling groceries and the vodka delivered once a month from the nearest town. All of the liquor (several cartons of it) was handed over to Stannitsky for distribution. He kept a list of how much each officer was allowed, always saving most for himself, of course. The officers grumbled about this, but they were afraid to protest openly. "What are a few bottles of vodka for a

whole month!" they muttered. Each of them wanted
two or three crates full!

Stannitsky liked to inspect the efficiency of the prisoners who worked in the forest. The soldiers guarding
the logging crew often warned them, "Warped is coming!" and the prisoners would throw themselves more
energetically into their work. If Warped caught anyone
resting or sitting by the fire, he immediately went to
work on the unfortunate one with his stick. Paradox-
ically, Stannitsky frequently brought packages of tea
for the work brigade, and sometimes even sat down
with them to drink a strong brew.

Labor camp life was not without its diversions. Card
games flourished against camp regulations. The inevitable gambling led to knifings and even murders. The
games were played late in the evening in the barracks.
Several prisoners would be posted at the entrance to
warn if a guard was approaching. When this happened,
the games stopped instantly, the cards magically disappeared, and the prisoners scurried to their bunks.

Camp card games were intensely serious affairs,
drawing many avid spectators into a tight circle around
the players. Losers settled their debts with cash (which
was officially forbidden in camp), cigarettes, food ra-
tions, or clothing. One prisoner lost the gold crowns on
his molars at cards. Right on the spot a large spike and
hammer were used to pry the crowns from his teeth!
But if their losses were very heavy and they could not
pay, their very lives could be forfeited.

One young convict, nicknamed "Vaska the Gambler," lost everything he owned: his money, prison
clothes, and boots. To regain his possessions, he offered
to continue playing—by betting the life of the warden!

It was agreed that if he won he would receive back all of his belongings; but if he lost, then he must kill Stannitsky. The card game resumed. Once again Vaska was unlucky. He retreated to his bunk, wearing only his shorts. He had already lost all of his clothing—and now he had lost the life of the camp commander! Vaska was beside himself with rage, cursing everything in the world. The victorious opponent gave Vaska a deadline: three days to clear his debt by murder, or else Vaska would be turned over to the camp homosexuals. Vaska determined to go to kill Warped.

Vaska the Gambler strode resolutely into Stannitsky's office. Tall, thin Vaska looked ridiculous in the short trousers and the skimpy jacket he had borrowed.

Vaska got right to the point.

"Warden, I lost your life at cards and must kill you!" announced this comical-looking intruder. His right hand remained in his pocket as though clutching something. Seated at his desk, Warped never quivered. He slowly raised his head and stared into the eyes of the prisoner. Their eyes locked as Vaska silently stared back. Moments passed. The tension mounted as the eyes of the warden and prisoner remained riveted.

"You've really done it, you miserable gambler!" Stannitsky finally roared. "Get back to the barracks instantly and win back my life at cards! I give you twenty-four hours to do it!" Stannitsky rose and pointed at the door. "Now take your hand out of your pocket and throw that knife into the waste basket!"

Vaska turned without a word. Taking his hand out of his pocket, he tossed a knife into the trash. Then he dashed out of the warden's office and sped back to the barracks.

The ensuing card game raged all day and all night. The next morning, a glowing Vaska, dressed in his own clothes, handed his winnings over to his pals to be hidden in case of a search. Later, Stannitsky ordered Vaska to his office. Two officers were also present.

"Tell us about your exploits, miserable gambler," commanded Warped.

"Citizen Warden, everything's all right! I won your life back," cheerfully announced the proud Vaska. He assumed, of course, that the warden would praise him.

"Scoundrel! Gambling on the life of the warden!" bellowed Warped. "Don't take cards into your hands if you can't play! Fifteen days in the punishment cell!" Then to the officers he barked, "After fifteen days, without returning him to the general zone, ship him to another labor camp!"

Vaska the Gambler crumbled. From a glowing hero, conqueror of the entire battalion of gamblers, he was reduced to a pitiful, shackled convict as he was marched under guard across the camp to solitary confinement.

"Don't take cards into your hands! Don't take cards into your hands if you can't play!" jeered the soldiers and officers as the prisoners watched.

Such was Chepichanka and such was its warden! And into that camp the Lord had sent three of his servants: Konshaubi Dzhangetov, Fyodor Makhovitsky, and me.

5

Three in Chepichanka

*T*he labor camp known as Chepichanka is situated in the northern part of the Permsky *oblast* (a political subdivision) about 250 miles north of the city of Solikamsk. The railway ends at Solikamsk and with it the only comfortable mode of transportation. Farther north of our camp there are no roads at all. Chepichanka is relatively small with only seven to eight hundred prisoners. It is designated an "ordinary regime" camp. Only those prisoners serving their first term are held here, although some of these sentences may be as long as ten to fifteen years.

Konshaubi Dzhangetov was the first of us three be-

lievers to be brought to Chepichanka in 1967. It was
January, when the frosts are most severe in the northern Urals. All of the warm clothes he had brought from
home were confiscated. He almost froze, wearing only
the light clothing issued to prisoners. The camp administration assigned him to a work brigade of about
thirty-five prisoners who were cutting and clearing a
path for a railway line through the dense forest. They
had to make their way more than two miles through
deep snow to the work area. Three soldiers with automatics guarded the prisoners with the help of a German
shepherd dog specially trained to attack at the soldiers'
orders.

Chepichanka was a place of constant, gnawing hunger. Prisoners were fed rotting fish cooked in a watery
"soup." The fish was often so decomposed and wormy
that it was impossible to use as food, even for prisoners.
Only then was it thrown out onto the garbage pile of
rotten cabbage, potatoes, carrots, and other refuse.
Meat, doled out in small quantities, was also foul and
rotting; unlike the rotten fish, however, it was soaked
in a manganese solution then boiled in so-called soup.

There were a number of horses at the camp used to
haul groceries and wood. In winter, they were reduced
to walking skeletons, their ribs barely covered by skin.
When not hard at work, they sometimes fed in despera-
tion on the icy heap of garbage. The pile grew throughout the winter and stood high in the middle of the camp
yard. The famished horses pawed at the congealed
mountain with their hooves, tearing out the frozen fish
and greedily devouring them, bones and all. Often dig-
ging around the same pile were a few convicts who had
become totally dehumanized. There were about twenty

of them—famished, unshaven, dirty, in torn, lice-ridden clothing—men who had given up on themselves. They would scrape out bits of rotten fish or cabbage with sticks and eat hungrily. Sometimes they pounced on chunks of fish turned over by the horses, their foraging rivals. It was a tragic sight, which could only be seen in a Soviet labor camp.

Those first days of hunger, cold and aching loneliness were the hardest for Konshaubi. Sometimes when his eyes were closed as he prayed before eating, someone would steal his metal bowl of watery soup. Often when he prayed in his barracks, a dirty boot would come hurtling toward him from some dark corner. An additional difficulty was communication. Having lived in the Caucasus all his life, Konshaubi spoke with the heavy accent of his district. The other prisoners, mostly Russians, could hardly understand a word he said. Circassian, his native tongue, does not even remotely resemble Russian. On top of all this, the officers ridiculed Konshaubi and his faith. "Ha! A Muslim—and a Baptist!" they would say derisively. "Dzhangetov, why do you believe in Christ? Christ is a myth! Here we are, Russians, and we don't believe in Christ. You're a Circassian, so how come you don't believe in Mohammed?"

Every cold, lonely day, he endured their scornful laughter and mockery. Konshaubi became completely discouraged. He had no Bible, not even a New Testament, and no one with whom he could share his griefs or have spiritual fellowship. How he yearned to hear from his family! Yet no mail was getting through to him, even though he faithfully sent a letter home every week. Only one other time had Konshaubi experienced such trials. It was when he first believed in Christ as a youth and was subjected to harsh persecution from his relatives and the other Muslims of his village. Konshaubi knew that the Lord had not abandoned him in loneliness and sorrow then, nor would he now.

In March, a new transport of prisoners arrived at Chepichanka. As usual, it was a big occasion for the inmates. Stannitsky himself met the new prisoners. He would loudly question some of them, "What are you in for? How long is your sentence?" From the prisoners' zone Konshaubi watched, too, hoping. *Surely the Lord will send at least one believer to this camp!* he thought.

Then he heard Stannitsky shout, "Makhovitsky, what are you sentenced for?"

The prisoner was a tall man with an open, pleasant expression on his face. His answer came quickly, cheerfully, in a resonant voice: "For faith in Jesus Christ!"

"What are you, a Baptist?" the warden queried.

"Yes!"

"Where from?"

"From Leningrad."

"So, it's the 'supreme pope' of Leningrad," guffawed Stannitsky. "Well, get into the camp. Your so-called 'brother in Christ,' Dzhangetov, is waiting for you."

Turning to the officer beside him he muttered, "What's wrong with the officials in Moscow, sending a second Baptist to our camp! Are they trying to create a Baptist zone here?"

With the arrival of Fyodor Makhovitsky, Konshaubi took fresh courage, and his heart grew light and joyful. At last he had a fellow believer standing with him, and he wanted to spend all of his free time with this new friend. Every evening after work they got together to talk, telling each other endless stories about their families and their churches.

Konshaubi and Fyodor lived in the same barracks. They prayed together openly, morning and evening. For some reason, boots were no longer thrown at them. Actually, the other prisoners lived their own lives, talking, arguing, shouting, and mostly ignoring the two believers. But if an officer came in while Konshaubi and Fyodor were praying, the other prisoners whispered loudly, "Sir, don't make any noise! The Baptists are praying!" And suddenly the officer, guards, and the seventy convicts stopped whatever they were doing and listened to the prayers of the two Christians. The officer generally became flustered, not knowing quite what to do. Then, shrugging his shoulders, he would quickly leave without disturbing them. As soon as he was gone, barracks life resumed its usual noisy rhythm. After praying, Konshaubi and Fyodor would be smugly informed that, "Just now an officer came in, but we managed him. If we hadn't, he'd still be here, picking on you about your praying!"

The faithful testimony of these men's lives became more and more apparent. One by one prisoners came to them for discussions about God. Others talked among themselves with wonder. "Baptists can't live without praying. They pray all the time—on the transports, before meals, in the morning when they get up, and at night before they sleep. Why are the Communists torturing them, sticking them into prison? The Baptists have the most genuine faith of all! If everyone behaved like them, there'd be no criminals or prisons or labor camps!"

Konshaubi was assigned to work as an orderly at the

punishment cell block, a small prison within the labor
camp, containing several tiny cells. Prisoners who com-
mitted a crime in camp, or simply violated a rule, were
confined to one of these cells for ten to fifteen days.
They were given only one small meal a day and an even
smaller daily ration of bread. The cells were cold, but
the soldiers took away all warm clothing, even the
prisoners' boots. A thin jacket was allowed only at
night. Prisoners in these cells slept on bare wooden
boards without any bedding. Konshaubi had to pass the
food to the prisoners, while under the strict supervision
of the soldiers. He also kept the fire going in the wood
stove, but it provided scant heat, and that only in the
immediate area.

At first many of the convicts wanted—yes, demanded—Konshaubi to secretly slip tobacco, cigarettes, matches, narcotics, and even knives to their
friends confined in the punishment cells. Konshaubi,
however, refused to do this despite their curses and
threats to get even.

"I'm a Christian," he said plainly, "and I'll never
touch tobacco, cigarettes, or narcotics, even if you kill
me! But I am willing to deliver any kind of food. I know
your friends are very hungry, and I'll take whatever
you want to share with them."

And so he did. When the prisoners gave him a piece of
bread with margarine or a little jam, Konshaubi
wrapped it in old newspaper and put it in the large
pocket of his jacket. Then, when no soldiers were nearby, he handed the packet into the cell.

All of the convicts in the camp soon knew that Konshaubi the Baptist would never touch narcotics or cig-

arettes, but was always ready to feed the hungry prisoners in the punishment cells. "That's the kind of strong faith the Baptists have!" asserted the prisoners to one another. They began to respect Konshaubi. Many even became friendly with him. They affectionately nicknamed him *Batya*, prison slang for "Father."

Working in the punishment cell block had its moments. Although the whole camp was infested with lice, the punishment cells had it the worst. The prisoners' padded vests were swarming with lice and nits. Konshaubi was entrusted with a small bottle of potent poison to deal with the problem.

"See that the poison doesn't get on your hands," the officer warned. "There'll be burns and ulceration!"

He told Konshaubi to use a brush and very carefully work the poison down the seams of the vests and jackets where the lice and nits were hidden. Konshaubi began this dangerous work in the soldiers' section of the barracks.

"Don't touch this bottle," he cautioned the soldiers. "There's poison in it!"

The convicts found out about the bottle and became quite interested. Narcotics and liquor were hard to come by, and some prisoners were ready to eat or drink anything to temporarily escape their wretchedness through a quick high. Antifreeze or even great quantities of toothpaste dissolved in water could do the trick. When they learned about the special poison for lice, a few prisoners decided to help themselves to the bottle. "If this poison were diluted with water," they told one another, "it might be an excellent substitute for vodka."

They knew Konshaubi would never give it to them, so they decided to steal it, seizing the opportunity when they were taken under guard to the lavatory.

Several hours passed before Konshaubi noticed that the bottle was gone. He became frantic. He checked with the soldiers, but they had not seen it. The mystery cleared up when they heard unusual sounds coming from one of the cells. They ran to see a most peculiar sight. The five prisoners were in an uproar. They were all singing, laughing, dancing, and leaping about. One man sat on the floor staring straight up at the ceiling, giggling noiselessly. Another kept trying to snatch an invisible object out of the air. Deep in a hallucinogenic ecstasy, all were oblivious to the soldiers who had entered their cell. The high was followed by the inevitable, horrible aftereffects. The men became extremely nauseated, screaming and moaning in agony. Konshaubi feared for their lives.

A medical orderly was called. He instructed that half a pail of water be poured down the throat of each of the miserable culprits to make them vomit. The next day the prisoners were lethargic, and the cell was very quiet. When they saw Konshaubi not long after, however, they grinned and said, "Forgive us, *Batya*, for swiping your little flask. What a high–like nothing else!" Then they added slyly, "Don't you have another little bottle on you?"

When I arrived at Chepichanka in April, my work assignment was as an electrician in the diesel electric power station situated in a small building in the camp work area. A month later the warden returned the papers which he had taken from me on my arrival. But true to his word, he did not return the Bible. Liberally sprinkled among my papers, however, were many handwritten quotations from the Scriptures, particularly from the Book of Psalms. Now at least I had these in my possession. During free time in the evenings, Konshaubi, Fyodor, and I read the Psalms, which Konshaubi painstakingly copied into his notebook. We especially loved Psalm 84: "How lovely is your tabernacle, O Lord of hosts! My soul longs, yes even faints for the courts of the Lord..." (*see* vv. 1, 2). Our souls were really longing for the fellowship of our churches. Each of us knew many verses from the Bible by heart, and we decided to write them all in Konshaubi's notebook. This lifted our spirits.

When the weather grew warmer, we would meet on Sundays beyond the barracks in an area dotted with large stumps, all that remained of the huge trees that had once graced those hills. There we would pray, sing hymns, and encourage each other with verses from God's Word written in our hearts and in Konshaubi's notebook.

By then Konshaubi was receiving many letters from his wife, Tonya, and friends. Tonya wrote that she was able to work only three or four hours a day because their six children were still young and in school. The church had not forsaken this family, but lovingly assisted the Dzhangetovs with food and clothing.

Tonya's letters often mentioned another of the family's good resources—their cow, Zoika. Before his arrest, Konshaubi took special care of Zoika. All the Dzhangetov children were growing up on Zoika's milk. She was a real treasure to the family, and the children loved

her. Now Zoika was left to Tonya. She often wrote
asking Konshaubi's advice about various problems:
Zoika was not eating well; Zoika looked a little sick; or
Zoika gave us a newborn calf. Konshaubi gave each
item much thought, and then replied in great detail,
explaining what to do in every situation.

The children's letters always refreshed Konshaubi,
especially those from the younger ones. They told him
about the worship services and youth meetings. Their
letters sparkled with the joy of the Lord and with a
vibrant faith. The two older sons, however, were a
source of anxiety to their father for they were indif-
ferent to the Word of God. Konshaubi never stopped
praying for them.

An elderly Christian man in the Caucasus used to
write regularly. He addressed his letters to both Konshaubi and to the camp commander, Stannitsky. A
typical letter from him went something like this:

> Dear brother in Christ, Konshaubi Bekirovich Dzhan-
> getov:
>
> This letter is written to you by your brother in the
> faith, Stepan. You must remember me. I'm 84 years old.
> You and I met and spoke together several times. Now
> you're imprisoned. The Lord sent you to the camp so
> that you would tell of God's love to all the officers there,
> and especially to the commander.
> Citizen Warden! God sent his own prophet, Kon-
> shaubi Bekirovich Dzhangetov, to your labor camp.
> Listen to his words about God and repent. Accept Christ
> into your heart, and you'll obtain eternal life!

Stepan would then literally command Konshaubi,

"Don't be fainthearted before the warden! Don't be silent! Go and read my letter to him and call him to repentance!"

Stannitsky, of course, saw these letters before Konshaubi did. After such a note, he asked with irritation, "Why is that old man so concerned about my soul? He'd better think about his own—pretty soon he'll be a hundred and have to die. Or maybe he wants to come here to my labor camp!"

Top: A hand-copied Bible displayed by Georgi Vins. Due to the great shortage of Bibles, many Christians are hand copying the entire Bible. Middle: Christian literature secretly brought in from the West is received with great joy and prepared for distribution. Bottom: In 1968 the Christian Publishing House printed its first New Testament on a small, homemade press. Because of the tremendous need for the printed Word, teams of young people dedicate themselves to printing Christian literature. If discovered by the police or KGB, the young people face certain arrest and imprisonment.

Denied permission by the authorities to have a prayer house, this
unregistered congregation meets outdoors.

The unregistered Leningrad church is full of children and young people.
Here they've gathered to celebrate the fall harvest (Thanksgiving).

Young people surround Mikhail Azarov following his release from prison in August 1985. Azarov was arrested with Fyodor Makhovitsky in 1981.

Members of the CEBC gathered for a meeting in 1987. Nearly all have been imprisoned at least once for their Christian activities.

Prisoners and martyrs who have suffered for the Gospel are remembered in this 1986 poster marking 25 years of revival in the Soviet Union. Every meeting carries a visible reminder to pray for the prisoners.

KGB agents frequently ransack believers' homes in search of Bibles, hymnals, and other Christian literature which is then confiscated.

Under heavy guard, a Christian prisoner is escorted to the courtroom to be tried.

Top: Fyodor Makhovitsky, pastor of the independent Baptist church in Leningrad, was arrested the second time in August, 1981. His daughter Svetlana was allowed to visit him for a few days at the strict regime prison camp where he served a five-year sentence. Middle: CEBC president Gennady Kryuchkov has been underground since 1970. Bottom: Pastor Dmitri Minyakov has served three prison terms for his ministry in the unregistered church.

Top: A soldier with a guard dog is followed by an officer during regular patrols around a strict regime labor camp. The sign on the post reads: "Closed Zone—Entrance Forbidden!" Middle: Twenty-six-year-old Sergei Dubitsky was arrested in October, 1985, with Konshaubi. Bottom: Adam and Tabitha Dubitsky, parents of Sergei. Mr. Dubitsky was arrested a few weeks after his son and sentenced to three years' strict regime, his fourth term for preaching the Gospel.

Concentration
camp scenes.

6

Communion in Camp

Special accommodations in a labor camp are provided for family visits, usually consisting of a room, a toilet, and a tiny kitchen. Bars cover the windows, and the door is locked and guarded. Family visits are generally permitted to last from one to three days, once or twice a year, depending on the type of labor camp. Because Chepichanka is an "ordinary regime" camp, two visits were allowed. (At a "strict regime" camp, only one family visit is allowed each year.)

The wives, children and mothers of the prisoners have a difficult journey to reach camps in the far North. Road and travel conditions are hazardous. Few of the convicts' wives will risk the journey. Wives of Christian prisoners, however, always try to visit their husbands, even at the most distant camps. They trust the Lord to give them safety, and depend on other believers to pray for them and help provide for the trip.

Fyodor had been at Chepichanka only two weeks when his wife, Klavdia, came from Leningrad for a three-day visit. She brought food and warm clothing for her husband. But the most important thing she brought was news of the church – that it was faithful and strong, and walking in obedience to the Lord despite persecution. Many young people were coming to Christ, she said, and children were attending meetings.

Not long after I arrived at Chepichanka, my wife, Nadia, came from Kiev for a two-day visit. The New Testament she brought for me was confiscated when guards searched her belongings. She had a large food parcel, including a tiny bottle of wine. She knew how much it would mean to us to be able to commemorate the Lord's Supper on Good Friday, only weeks away.

Now all we needed was a quiet place to hold our communion service. We considered the doctor's office which often stood empty because he only came to Chepichanka a few days two or three times a year. Next to the office was a small ward for the sick. The ward contained five or six ordinary metal cots. No one had been in the ward for some time, not because everyone was healthy, but simply because for several months the doctor had not appeared. Those who had been in the ward were either back in their zones or dead. No one could be sent to the sick ward without the absent doctor's orders.

A medical orderly, who was one of the prisoners, was

in charge of the empty ward and the doctor's office. He allowed Konshaubi, Fyodor, and me to celebrate the Lord's Supper there. With joyful hearts, we met on Good Friday. We brought a hunk of prisoners' black bread and placed the tiny bottle of wine and an empty glass on a table. Fyodor and Konshaubi asked me to lead in this remembrance of our Lord's suffering and death. We prayed and asked God to protect our small worship service from disruptions. This unusual communion service was very precious to us, since none of us had participated in the Lord's Supper since our arrests. For me, it was over a year; for Konshaubi and Fyodor, almost as long.

We felt a special significance in this ordinance. The Lord had instituted it just before his own arrest, when he faced the suffering and torture of death on the cross. Now he had given us, his followers, the privilege of experiencing bonds for his holy name. We felt the forces of atheism, not just the philosophy, but State atheism and all of its machinery at war to destroy our faith in God and to separate us from the love of God. But as we prayed together that day, our hearts were again restored in the assurance that "in all these things we are more than conquerors through him that loved us" (Romans 8:37, KJV).

I took the bread and spoke the words of our Lord by heart, "Take, eat: this is my body, which is broken for you: this do in remembrance of me." I prayed and, breaking the bread into three portions, offered one to each brother. Then I poured the wine. Holding it in my hand, I said softly, "This cup is the new testament of my blood; this do ye in remembrance of me." I passed the glass to Brother Fyodor, who prayed over the wine.

Then we drank, just a few drops each. We knelt together and thanked the Lord for his great sacrifice of love on the cross of Golgotha, for salvation and eternal life given to us through his suffering, death, and glorious resurrection. Then quietly, brokenly, with overflowing hearts, we sang a hymn of thanksgiving and praise to our lovely Redeemer.

Our service was over. It had been a rare and precious hour in prison conditions. We were so grateful to the Lord that no one had hindered us and that he had made it possible for us to unite in this remembrance of his death "Till he come!"

7

A Double Miracle

*B*ehold, how good and how pleasant it is for brethren to dwell together in unity!" (Psalm 133:1, KJV). Yes, it was good for the three of us to be together in the northern labor camp. But Fyodor and I noticed that Konshaubi was growing despondent. He longed for his wife and children.

"Konshaubi, why can't Tonya come here to visit you?" Fyodor asked one day.

"The journey from Ust-Dzheguta is long," answered Konshaubi sadly. "And who will stay at home with our children?"

"Write a letter to the men at your church," we

advised him. "They will help Tonya make the trip here to you."

So Konshaubi wrote to his church and to his wife. Soon he received a reply with the good news that she would soon be arriving. Konshaubi's joy was boundless! He went about his duties cheerily, always smiling. The warden allowed a three-day visit and officially set the date.

Several weeks later Tonya finally arrived. I guessed what had happened the day I returned from work and saw a beaming Konshaubi in excited conversation with Fyodor. "Tonya is here!" Konshaubi shouted to me. Fyodor had found out first, since he worked in the administration building.

I embraced him. "I'm so glad for you, my brother! When does your visit begin?"

"I'm just going to the officer now to find out," and Konshaubi hurried to the guard's station.

The next three days Konshaubi was not with us in the barracks. Fyodor and I were happy that the Lord had made it possible to see Tonya after nearly a year of separation. We awaited his return impatiently. We wanted to hear news of our brothers and sisters in the Caucasus, of Konshaubi's church in Ust-Dzheguta, and of his children, and all his family. And as we waited, we clung to another unspoken hope. Perhaps, just perhaps, this time the longed-for New Testament would come through. Tonya would bring one, of course, but would it be confiscated? All three of us had been praying about this with great urgency over the past weeks.

Toward evening on the second day of Tonya's visit, Fyodor and I walked up to the visitor's building. One of the windows overlooked our zone. Outside were the usual iron bars. Two-thirds of the window was covered with white paint, but the top part was clean, clear glass enabling us to see inside. Tonya and Konshaubi saw us and waved. We could not speak to them, of course, but we smiled back and raised our hands toward heaven, our permanent home, where there will be no prisons and labor camps, no sorrows, and no more separations.

Konshaubi returned from his visit with mixed emotions. He was sad at parting with Tonya, but his eyes were twinkling. Obviously, he was awaiting an opportunity to tell us something important. We looked for a quiet spot where we could talk.

"Do you have some good news for us?" I finally asked, almost afraid to put our wish into words.

Konshaubi glanced about. "Yes—a New Testament!" He barely breathed the words.

"Praise the Lord!" Fyodor and I whispered from the depths of our hearts. Our prayers had been answered! How much we had yearned for God's Word! For us it was a double miracle: not only was Tonya able to bring the New Testament into the visitor's quarters, but Konshaubi had managed to get it into the camp zone. Only God could have done that!

8

Those with Whom We Shared

Keeping food in the barracks was impossible. The convicts stole bread even from one another. That is why a special "food locker," a small room with bars on the windows and a sturdy metal door, was always kept bolted shut. From six o'clock in the morning until ten o'clock at night, this locker was attended by a prisoner appointed by the officials. There the prisoners kept all their food parcels, including any extra bread they accumulated. The "keeper" handed food to the prisoners through a small window in the door of the locker. If you had a piece of salt pork, a packet of margarine, or a can of jam in the locker, you could get it out, take what you wanted, and return the remainder for safekeeping. Of course you must share some of your goods with the keeper as a reward for his diligent watch over your groceries. Labor camp life was riddled with such unwritten laws.

Many prisoners never received food parcels. Konshaubi, Fyodor, and I always shared any food given to us by our wives with those prisoners. We tried to help some on a steady basis, a little at a time. I especially remember one tall, thin young fellow of about twenty from the city of Tashkent. He had a dark, long face with large, expressive eyes. The convicts called him "Djaga." He was constantly famished. As a child, he was a homeless street urchin. Now he was imprisoned for petty thievery. His father was an Uzbek, and his mother a Jewess. He sang well, constantly repeating the same sad song about "Mother."

Djaga looked shy and timid. With a soft voice he would ask, "Do you have an extra little piece of bread?" We tried to help Djaga by giving him not only food, but also any clothing we could spare.

Then there was Sergei, from Moscow, who seemed particularly distressed. Like Djaga, he was always very hungry. He was emaciated, just skin and bones. He did not have a long sentence, he said, only a year for being in a drunken brawl in a Moscow subway. Sergei did the general maintenance in the prisoners' barracks as well as various repairs in the administration buildings. His clothes were always stained with paint and calcimine. He always looked frightened but remained secretive and silent. The other prisoners did not like him. Suspiciously they would ask, "Who were you in Moscow?

Where did you work? You don't look like an ordinary person."

Sometimes prisoners would beat Sergei, after which he would furtively slink away. We could see that he suffered from malnutrition, loneliness, and from some great personal anxiety. We tried to befriend Sergei, encouraging him and sharing our bread, margarine, and occasionally salt pork. When we spoke to him about God, he listened attentively and patiently, but seldom asked questions. We did not know Sergei's real attitude regarding faith in God; perhaps he was so attentive out of simple courtesy.

When his sentence was nearly completed, Sergei said to me, "On the last day of my term, just before I'm released, I want to speak to you privately."

On his last day at Chepichanka, Sergei came into our barracks and said good-bye to Fyodor and Konshaubi, thanking them for their help. "In this camp only you are real people in the full sense of the word!" said Sergei in parting. Then he drew me aside to the end of our section.

"Nobody in camp knows who I am except the officer for special camp affairs," he whispered earnestly. "I am in this camp of criminals by accident. I was not supposed to be held here. In Moscow I was an officer in the militia with the rank of major. I was involved in a confrontation in the subway with a young man. I was drunk and hit him. It was completely my fault. It turned out that he was a relative of the State Minister for Internal Affairs, and that's why I'm here. This is his revenge. Usually we workers of the militia are held in our own special labor camps where there are no criminals. If the prisoners here knew who I was, I would be murdered some night!" Sergei spoke with bitterness. Then he continued.

"I am very thankful to you believers for your warm attitude toward me—not just for the bread and salt pork, but for your humane behavior to me, a misfit!" Almost in tears, Sergei forced out the next words. "I, as a major in the militia, took part in the breaking up of Baptist meetings in the Moscow area. I arrested your brothers in the faith. I scorned and ridiculed them. And now, here in this place, no one helped me except you believers!"

"Sergei, when you return to Moscow, find the group of believers whom you persecuted and start going to their meetings," I pleaded. "You need Christ! You need salvation!"

I gripped his hand in a firm handshake. "I will pray for you, Sergei, all my life," I promised as we parted.

Another young prisoner with whom I became acquainted was Victor. We met during one of the temporary prison stops while being transported from Moscow to Chepichanka. During that trip, Victor had a terrible toothache. There was probably an abcess below the tooth, as one cheek was badly swollen. He could neither eat nor sleep because of the pain. He was growing weak, and I tried to help him gain a little strength by giving him some sweetened tea. Later, when the swelling subsided, Victor became very interested in my view of life, particularly my faith in God. After we arrived at Chepichanka, I introduced him to Fyodor and Konshaubi. When we got the New Testament, Victor was among the first to read it. Before long, he was praying with us. All in all, about six months after Konshaubi, Fyodor and I arrived at camp, there were more than ten people who were very close to faith in God, but the only one who openly prayed with us was Victor.

This did not go unnoticed by the camp administration. A worried Warden Stannitsky told the officers, "If we don't take decisive measures, in another six months half the camp will be Baptists!" Of course he was exaggerating. But it was obvious that the atheists were very disturbed. Every day lively discussions would spring up regarding faith in God.

One prisoner who often joined in these discussions was in the bunk next to mine. Mikhail Kryuchkov came from Moscow. He, too, had been on the transport with me. I met him at the beginning of our journey. About a hundred of us prisoners had already been divided into groups and loaded into the convicts' section of the train. The officers were shouting out the names of the prisoners on their lists, checking those present. Each prisoner had to respond with his name, patronymic, year of birth, and Article of the Criminal Code under which he was sentenced.

Suddenly an officer called, "Kryuchkov!" Someone in a neighboring section replied but his words were muffled by distance and the general commotion. My heart leaped upon hearing the familiar surname. Could it possibly be Gennady Kryuchkov, my brother in the Lord with whom I'd been arrested and sentenced in Moscow?

Later, when the train moved forward and everyone gradually settled down, I tried to find out where "Kryuchkov" was. I waited until the soldier in the corridor had moved away and then I shouted, "Kryuchkov, Gennady!" But it was an unfamiliar voice which responded, "Kryuchkov, Mikhail. And who are you?"

I gave my name, but this Kryuchkov did not know me. During the long transit, we became acquainted at the stopover prisons. Mikhail Kryuchkov was a friendly, easygoing man of about thirty-three. He had been arrested and sentenced for theft. I told him about Gennady Kryuchkov and of our arrest and trial because of our faith in God.

In Chepichanka, Mikhail began reading the New Testament and seemed to be close to finding God. Fyodor would sometimes say to him, "Oh, Misha, Misha, what a good surname you have! How did you become a convict?" He said it very tenderly, as a father would. Mikhail was not offended and he continued to ask many questions about the way of salvation.

9

The Moscow Commission

*E*arly in July of 1967, we heard that a commission from the Ministry of Internal Affairs (MVD) was coming from Moscow. All prisoners were immediately sent to the camp bathhouses and issued clean underclothing. Overgrown beards were shaved. The camp zone was cleaned and tidied up. A shipment of fresh sand was spread among the pathways throughout the camp. Flower beds were prepared and planted. In the dining hall, the flies that buzzed in thousands over the prisoners' food were exterminated. The remains of the garbage pile outside the kitchen disappeared and sand was poured over the area. The horses had long since lost interest in the rotten fish, thanks to the abundance of lush, green grass all around. The horses themselves seemed younger, taller, heavier, and full of new vigor and life. They proudly tossed their freshly combed manes and would nip or kick any unwary idler. It was as though they remembered that these were the ones who had stolen the food right out from under their hooves during the harsh winter.

Large billboards suddenly appeared on the walls of the barracks. Each displayed a portrait of Lenin and bold, patriotic slogans such as:

THE TEACHINGS OF LENIN ARE TRUTH AND THERE-FORE ETERNAL!

THE PARTY AND THE PEOPLE ARE ONE!

ON TO FREEDOM WITH A CLEAR CONSCIENCE!

LET'S GIVE OUR HOMELAND MORE TIMBER!

This was 1967 and the jubilee celebrations marking fifty years of Soviet rule were fast approaching. The prisoners were in great anticipation that amnesty would free many of them.

After its long-anticipated arrival, the commission from Moscow was in the camp only one day. Members of the commission strolled about on the fresh sand, gazing at the flowers, peeping into the prisoners' neat barracks, and visiting the now-immaculate dining hall. They also summoned several prisoners for interviews. Fyodor was among them.

The talks were held in Warden Stannitsky's office.

Besides the members of the Moscow commission, Stan-nitsky and two or three camp officers were also present. The chairman of the commission politely introduced himself as a colonel with the MVD and said to Fyodor, "You, no doubt, know that amnesty is likely this year for some of the prisoners on account of the great Fiftieth Anniversary of Soviet power?"

Yes, said Fyodor, he knew.

"And you, personally, do you anticipate that you will be freed by this amnesty?" asked the colonel.

Fyodor shrugged doubtfully. "I don't know."

The colonel turned to Stannitsky. "How many Baptists do you have in this camp?"

Warped shifted uncomfortably. "They sent us three," he answered, "but today there are more of them in the camp. I'd say about ten or fifteen. Makhovitsky and his friends are carrying on active religious propaganda work in the camp. I've already informed the ministry in Moscow of this situation. I'm waiting for directions regarding what to do with them."

The colonel turned back to Fyodor. "Makhovitsky, why do you busy yourself with religious propaganda in camp?" he asked. "Do you want to get another prison term? I've been informed that you and your so-called 'brothers in faith' pray in the barracks and force your religious beliefs on other prisoners." The colonel's expression hardened. "If you don't cease praying, you'll never get any amnesty!"

"We cannot stop praying; this is our life and our faith in God," calmly replied Fyodor. "It is because of our faith that we are here."

"Either prayer or freedom—choose!" Stannitsky interrupted.

Fyodor didn't hesitate. "I will continue to pray to God!"

Visibly irritated, the colonel said, "This camp is a State institution. The church is separate from the State by law. You don't have the right to pray in your barracks."

"Then where may we pray?" quietly asked Fyodor.

"In the toilet!" bellowed the Moscow colonel, his face red with anger.

Another commission member spoke up. "If you don't quit your praying and your preaching, we'll send you to other, much worse labor camps! When you're freed, pray at home."

"We have prayed and will continue to pray beside our bunks in the barracks," Fyodor said evenly. "You deprived us of our liberty and tore us away from our wives and children. You brought us here to this camp in the far North; now our bunks in the barracks are our homes, and we pray there."

The enraged colonel sputtered, "We'll send you even farther north!"

"Citizen Colonel, there is no road farther north. Only the Arctic Ocean is beyond. If you take us to another camp, it will have to be to the south," Fyodor softly answered.

"Warden, assign this man to do the most difficult work!" ordered the colonel. Then to Fyodor he blurted, "This conversation is finished! You may go."

As Fyodor was leaving the office the colonel added, "Makhovitsky, consider the amnesty! Your freedom is in your own hands. Your children and wife are waiting for you."

Fyodor remained silent as he continued out the door.

10

Our Last Days Together

After the Moscow commission left, Stannitsky began summoning prisoners for discussions, especially those who had often been seen talking to us. He promised each one a speedy release through the amnesty about to be proclaimed if they would repudiate all connections with us. Meanwhile, Fyodor was transferred to the building brigade, putting up houses in the nearby settlement.

Not long afterward, an officer who secretly sympathized with us told Konshaubi, "In two days, the three of you will be out of here, all to different camps."

When we heard this, we wondered what would become of those in the camp who were seeking Christ so earnestly. We began praying, "Lord, please leave at least one of us in this camp in order to continue the work with these men who are so close to finding you!"

The very next day, the officer on guard ordered Konshaubi, Fyodor, and me to return all camp property (mattress, blanket, pillow, metal soup bowl) and to prepare for transit.

We decided to spend that evening in a secret prayer meeting with all of the prisoners who were drawing very near to God. One of our friends, a new Christian, worked in the laundry section of the camp. It was quite a large, airy building. Ten of us gathered there: Fyodor, Konshaubi, myself, and seven others. I was asked to lead the meeting. This was the first time we had all come together for a "service." I held the precious New Testament in my hands. Everyone present was already familiar with this Holy Book. We prayed. Konshaubi, Fyodor, and I each gave a brief, encouraging message. Our new friends became very sad when I told them of the coming separation.

"We will always pray for each one of you," I said. "We believe that the Lord will send you his minister. You will not be left as orphans. We are leaving this New Testament for you, and we have chosen one of you to be responsible for your little group, the future camp church. We've decided, Mikhail, to pass the New Testament on to you, and to entrust to you the spiritual nurturing of this group and of the whole camp. The Lord will never leave you nor forsake you."

I handed Mikhail the New Testament and prayed in closing. Then, with great emotion, we said good-bye to one another. One by one we slipped out and returned to our various barracks.

The next morning, Konshaubi, Fyodor, and I were summoned to the guards' room where we were thoroughly searched. Then, under guard, the three of us were led out of the camp. We had walked only about forty or fifty feet when one of the soldiers shouted, "Dzhangetov, get back into the camp! You're staying here!"

Startled, Fyodor and I also stopped. What happened? Why? The questions raced through our minds. The officer came and touched Konshaubi's shoulder. "Let's go—back to the camp!"

Konshaubi was bewildered. Just a moment ago, he thought he was leaving Chepichanka for good. Now he was going back. We were all stunned. Fyodor recovered first.

"Konshaubi!" he whispered. "The Lord is leaving you in the camp! You are the one who is needed here!"

Fyodor could say no more. The soldiers were impatient. "What are you standing around for? Let's go!"

One quick embrace, then we watched as Konshaubi was led back through the massive gates. The soldiers took Fyodor and me to the waiting transport. As we climbed on, we were torn between joy at our answered prayers and deep sadness at parting with our brother.

"Till we meet again, Konshaubi, may the
Lord keep you!"

11

Reunion and Farewell

Konshaubi Dzhangetov was released in September 1969 from his first imprisonment. I had already been freed, as had Fyodor Makhovitsky, whose term was only two years. After his release, Konshaubi visited Leningrad where Fyodor pastored the unregistered church. It was a joyous meeting for these two men who had served the Lord together in a distant camp in the North.

I myself didn't see Konshaubi again until 1972, when the ministers in the Caucasus region had gathered for a secret meeting. As a representative of the Council of Evangelical Baptist Churches, I'd been invited to pre-

sent a general overview of the Lord's work in the Soviet
Union. The meeting was to last one night. About one
hundred leaders from the Evangelical Christian Baptist churches in the Caucasus had come. I was fairly
certain that Konshaubi would be there, too, and I was
eager to see him. Sure enough, I spotted him.

What a reunion! Together we reminisced about how
he, Fyodor, and I had sat on tree stumps as we prayed,
sang, and shared what we were going through and our
joy in the Lord. And now we were together again! But
the meeting soon began, and there was little time for
private conversation.

Several brothers and I had brought a large quantity
of Christian literature, newly arrived from the West—
Bibles, New Testaments, concordances, and several
Bible commentaries. This is extremely precious literature for believers in the Soviet Union, a country without a single store where you can buy a Bible or religious
literature. I had prepared for Konshaubi a special gift
of a Bible, concordance, Bible dictionary, and several
other books. He was overjoyed to receive them!

After the meeting, Konshaubi and I talked a little
more. For him, he said, prison camp had been a tremendous spiritual school, a school of experience, patience,
and hoping in the Lord. He also shared his burden for
his own people, the Circassians. He asked me to pray
for his ministry to his native people.

We embraced and said good-bye, not realizing that
we would probably never again see each other on earth.
That last meeting with Konshaubi remains vivid in my
mind even today, more than fifteen years later. The
following year, in 1973, Konshaubi was again arrested

and sentenced to three years' imprisonment, this time to a camp in the far North near Archangelsk.

I was able to visit Konshaubi's wife and family at their home that year. Tonya told me sadly that the books I had given Konshaubi were confiscated when he was arrested. This is nothing new for believers in the persecuted church. The authorities often search their homes and seize all religious literature. We prayed together that the Lord would help Konshaubi walk his path of testing. As we said farewell, I asked Tonya to give my warmest greetings to her husband at their next visit.

In 1976, when Konshaubi returned home from his second term of imprisonment, I was serving a ten-year sentence in Yakutia, eastern Siberia. Because I was exiled to the United States in 1979, I did not see Konshaubi again. On October 30, 1985, Konshaubi Dzhangetov was arrested for the third time, and sentenced to three more years of imprisonment.

I ask all who love the Lord and his persecuted church to remember Konshaubi Bekirovich Dzhangetov in your prayers. I believe in the power of prayer. I believe that prayer can move mountains and overcome all obstacles. Dear Christian reader, please pray faithfully for Konshaubi's wife, Tonya, his six children, and his church in Ust-Dzheguta.

12

Fyodor Makhovitsky

What became of Fyodor Makhovitsky and the unregistered church he pastored in Leningrad?

In 1967 we were taken from Chepichanka to separate camps about five hundred kilometers south—I to the Anyusha camp and Fyodor to the Gashkova camp. The two camps were about seventy kilometers apart. Both were lumber camps. Not long after our transfer, Gashkova was closed, and all the prisoners were moved. About two hundred were brought to my camp. How eagerly I anticipated Fyodor's arrival! As the prisoners were unloaded, I searched for his cheerful face.

Several prisoners from Gashkova found me and said,

"Your friend Makhovitsky was in our group, but about twenty kilometers from here he was taken off the train. He was the only one taken off."

My heart was grieved, but I knew very well why the authorities didn't want us to be in this camp together. They want believers to be alone in order to make things harder for them.

Later a prisoner came to me and said, "I have a gift for you from Makhovitsky. He had a little New Testament with him on the train. He was afraid they wouldn't let him into this camp, so he gave it to me and told me to give it to you."

I was deeply touched that Fyodor had been so concerned about me. He had given me the most precious treasure that a Christian in prison can have—God's Word! I was grateful to him and to the Lord for this little New Testament. It was a tremendous encouragement to me during my prison term.

Fyodor Makhovitsky was taken to a camp near Leningrad where he served the last months of his two-year term. He was released in 1968. His church joyfully welcomed him home. The unregistered church in Leningrad was growing spiritually and increasing in numbers. In the early 1980s, it had approximately three hundred members, seventy percent of whom were young people between the ages of fifteen and thirty.

The authorities, of course, were becoming increasingly concerned about this independent church, which based its ministry on the gospel. They prepared to strike a blow against it. On August 13, 1981, five searches were conducted in the apartments of believers in Leningrad. As usual, all Bibles and other Christian books were confiscated. On August 14, 1981, Pastor

Fyodor Makhovitsky, then fifty, and evangelist Mikhail Aleksandrovich Azarov, then forty-four, were arrested. They were taken to the infamous Kresty prison in Leningrad, where they were held for six months before being brought to trial.

(It must be noted that in the Soviet Union, prisoners are not released on bond. Once a man is arrested, he is held in strict isolation until his trial. He is given no legal counsel or defense. He may not communicate with his family through letters or by telephone. He has no way of knowing what is going on in the outside world; likewise, the family has no information about their father, husband, or son. Makhovitsky and Azarov were held incommunicado until their trial.)

A third man, fifty-four-year-old Vladimir Protsenko, was also on trial with them for allowing his home to be used for regular worship services. All three men were convicted and sentenced: Makhovitsky to five years' strict regime and confiscation of property; Azarov to four years' normal regime (it was his first term) and confiscation of property; and Protsenko to three years' imprisonment and confiscation of his house.

Thus the Leningrad congregation was deprived, not only of three brothers, two of whom were ministers, but also of its church building.

Today the Leningrad congregation usually meets in the forest outside of the city. The conditions are difficult. In the winter it is cold and snowy. In the spring, summer, and fall it rains. But the church is very much alive—and the authorities continue their attacks. On January 29, 1986, four men from the unregistered Leningrad church were put on trial: Pastor Vladimir Filippov (who took Pastor Makhovitsky's place when he was

imprisoned), his son Andrei Filippov, Veniamin Yef-
remov, and Stanislav Chudakov. All were sentenced;
Pastor Filippov received the harshest punishment of
four years' strict regime.

Every year, thousands of foreign tourists visit Leningrad, a city of ten million people. They are comfortably
escorted to the city's only registered Baptist church.
Smiling guides proudly inform them that believers in
Russia face no special hardships and enjoy complete
religious freedom. Few visitors notice the absence of
children and young people in the church. Even fewer
wonder why there is but one such congregation. Carefully concealed are such facts as three hundred believers in Leningrad who are deprived of their church
building, their pastors imprisoned.

Brothers Azarov and Protsenko have finished their
terms and returned home. Yet the attacks against the
Leningrad church persist. On August 16, 1986, young
believers throughout the Soviet Union were traveling
to Leningrad for a youth rally in a nearby forest. Hun-
dreds never arrived, having been pulled off of trains by
police enroute. Only about two hundred fifty made it to
the meeting site, where many of them were brutally
attacked by seven hundred KGB agents and policemen.

Fyodor Makhovitsky was released in the middle of
August 1986. Many believers gathered at the airport
to meet him. After waiting several hours, airport officials announced that the plane had been delayed and
wouldn't arrive that evening; they may as well go
home. They decided to wait anyway. And Pastor Makhovitsky did finally arrive that very evening. Tears and
great joy mingled freely as they welcomed their beloved

pastor home. They prayed together right in the airport. And thus began a new chapter in the life of Fyodor Makhovitsky, as he continued tirelessly and fearlessly to work for the Lord.

13

Konshaubi's
Third Trial

*O*n October 30, 1985, fifty-six-year-old Konshaubi Dzhangetov was arrested for the third time, together with twenty-six-year-old Sergei Dubitsky. Their five-day trial took place in December (10, 11, 16, 17, 18) 1985 in Cherkessk, Stavropolsky krai. Christians present at the trial provided the following excerpts of the proceedings:

Judge: "Defendant Dzhangetov! Have you ever been at gatherings of unregistered Baptists?"

Dzhangetov: "Yes, I attend worship services because I am a Christian."

Judge: "Did you urge people to disregard Soviet laws concerning cults?"

Dzhangetov: "I urged people to repent before God! (Smiling kindly, he looked at the judges.) Citizen judges, you also should repent before God! The Lord loves you! He wants to give you salvation and eternal life. Leave the sinful life and repent before God!"

Judge: "Dzhangetov! This is neither a prayer house nor a gathering of believers; this is a court! Knock off the sermon! Now tell me, how many people attend your worship services? How many children are at the meetings?"

Dzhangetov: "Many!"

Judge: "Be specific."

Dzhangetov: "I didn't count, but God knows!"

Judge: "And where do you get religious literature? Who brings it to you?"

Dzhangetov: "I am not accountable to the court in this matter."

Judge: "Where is the Christian Publishing House located?"

Dzhangetov: "The Christian Publishing House is located wherever God has determined."

Judge: "Why is there no price on the books of the Christian Publishing House?"

Dzhangetov: "The price isn't indicated because the Bible is priceless! It is the Book of Books, more precious than gold!"

Judge: "What is your opinion of the *Legislation Regarding Religious Cults*?"

Dzhangetov: "I don't agree with the *Legislation Regarding Religious Cults* since it contradicts the Bible."

Judge: "Dzhangetov! Are you by nationality Circassian?"

Dzhangetov: "Yes, I'm Circassian."

Judge: "How is it that you, being Circassian, changed from your Muslim faith to the Christian faith?"

Dzhangetov: "Christ is the Savior of all people. He died on Golgotha's cross for me. But Mohammed didn't die for me and didn't rise again."

Judge: "Do you know Vins?"

Dzhangetov: "Yes, I know him."

Judge: "And where did you meet Vins?"

Dzhangetov: "I met Georgi Petrovich Vins in 1967 in the Urals where we both were serving sentences as prisoners in a camp."

The judge questioned Dubitsky.

Judge: "Tell me, defendant Dubitsky, have you spread slanderous fabrications concerning believers Nikolai Khmara and Ivan Moiseyev?"

Dubitsky: "At meetings of believers I told of the martyrs' deaths of Baptist believers—about Nikolai Khmara, who was killed in prison, and about the soldier Ivan Moiseyev, who was killed in the army. Even today many believers suffer bonds for the name of the Lord."

Judge: "That's slander! In our country, no one is persecuted for his faith!"

Dubitsky: "This is not slander; it's reality! I know the relatives of prisoners, their wives, their mothers, their children, whose husbands, sons, and fathers even today are in prison for faith in God! For many years prison has served as a permanent place of residence for many Christians."

In the trial, witnesses appeared, mostly school-

teachers. They said that, being members of city com-
missions monitoring the observance of the *Legislation
Regarding Religious Cults*, they had attended meetings
of believers. One of the witnesses testified:

"At the Baptist meetings there were many children.
We saw twelve- and thirteen-year-olds praying together with adults. Once we were at a special meeting
called 'Harvest Holiday' where everything had been
beautifully decorated: flowers, fruit, and vegetables
were artistically arranged. When we entered, Dzhangetov was preaching. He urged the listeners to repent and
to serve God."

At the trial, Eidarov, a Circassian truck driver, also
appeared as a witness. He recounted:

"When I started to drive the truck away from the
motor pool, Dzhangetov ran toward the truck, handed
me two small books through my open window and said,
'Here, read these.' The supervisor of the motor pool was
with me. I took one book, my supervisor took the other.
The books were in the Circassian language. I started to
read the book at home that evening but I didn't understand it. It was all about God. . . . In the morning, my
brother took the book to the Party committee and told
them that the supervisor of the motor pool had one, too.
The Party committee took the other book from the
supervisor. Then they started calling us in for discussions both at the Party committee at work and at the
regional Party committee in Ust-Dzheguta."

Judge: "What are the titles of these books that
Dzhangetov gave you?"

Witness Eidarov: "*Inzhil*, in Circassian."

Judge: "And what does that mean in Russian?"

Someone shouted out: "Suffer!"

But Dzhangetov asked the judge for permission to explain the title and the judge complied.

Dzhangetov: "The word *inzhil* means 'good news.' This is a book about Jesus Christ, who died for all people, including Circassians. (Dzhangetov turned to the witness Eidarov:) I'm very sorry that you didn't finish reading this book about Jesus Christ."

Then the public prosecutor appeared with the speech for the prosecution. In his indictment he said:

"Under the guise of religious ceremonies, the illegal Evangelical Christian Baptist communities became more active in the cities of Karachayevsk, Cherkessk, and Ust-Dzheguta. Evidence shows that, under the direction of the Council of Evangelical Baptist Churches [CEBC], Dubitsky and Dzhangetov told believers not to submit to Soviet laws and they drew children into Baptist society.

"In particular, Dzhangetov, from 1981 through 1985, and Dubitsky, from 1983 through 1985, organized large, illegal assemblies three times. The defendants appeared with slanderous propaganda; intentionally, they spread libel according to the instructions of the CEBC.

"The *Bulletin* of the Council of Prisoners' Relatives, published in 1980 under the guise of religion, reports information concerning Baptist convicts in our country.

"On August 30 in the house of Alentyev, in the presence of two hundred people, Dzhangetov appealed for prayer for those who are in prison. In the home of Burkakov, Dzhangetov appeared with slanderous propaganda and claimed that without faith in God there is no life, and that the fact that many scientists believe in God is concealed from young people. On May 8, in the city of Cherkessk at the meeting of the unregistered community, they appealed for prayer for those suffering for their faith. And the believers, in ecstasy, fell to their knees and prayed.

"In his slanderous fabrications, Dubitsky exceeded Dzhangetov. In Karachayevsk, Dubitsky claimed that the persecution of believers had intensified. He spoke of Khmara, Minyakov, and Moiseyev. On July 28, 1985, Dubitsky organized and actively participated in the collective praying of children.

"In December of 1984 and March of 1985, great quantities of illegal literature were removed from the defendants: the magazine *Herald of Truth*, lists of prisoners, and *Bulletin*. This literature contains false fabrications of Soviet life. Everyone must understand that today Dubitsky and Dzhangetov are being tried not for their faith, but for slander and for systematically teaching religion to children. Believers write declarations and petitions. The signature of defendant Dubitsky under exhibit No. 43 appears on one joint petition-declaration.

"Dzhangetov, for the whole period of his activities, has already been convicted twice of breaking the law; Dubitsky has already been taken to the police station two times.

"I request that the court consider aggravating circumstances, the fact that their activities represent increased danger to society and the Soviet government."

In their defense, Konshaubi Bekirovich Dzhangetov and Sergei Adamovich Dubitsky both maintained that the literature confiscated from them did not contain libel, that the official examination by "experts" had been biased, and that they personally had never slandered the Soviet government.

Dzhangetov and Dubitsky cited a few facts of persecution of believers. They also stated that the *Legislation Regarding Religious Cults* contradicts the Bible and even the Constitution of the U.S.S.R.

Dzhangetov's final statement: "Even if I am deprived of freedom, I remain free on the inside before people and before you, citizen judges. You haven't conducted a proper, just, judicial investigation. This will remain on your conscience, but I forgive you of everything!"

Dubitsky's final statement: "I'm glad that I'm in this courtroom not as an aggressor, thief, or murderer. I already learned in prison that the greatest judge is one's own conscience. My conscience has never condemned me for my faith in God. Christ said, 'They have persecuted Me, they will also persecute you. . . .' 'All that will live godly in Christ Jesus shall suffer persecution.' I'm glad for my brotherhood in Christ, which goes forth for Christ in spite of persecution.

"I read a book entitled *From the Community Toward the Church*, which I bought at Dom Knigi [Book House]. The author writes that the persecution of Christians never gave and never will give the desired results. For us with Christ, even in prison there is freedom. Without Christ, even in freedom there is prison.

"I have been sick many years. Ever since childhood I have been on the medical records of both the endocrinologist and the internist. But I know it's useless to ask you to consider my health. But I want to say to my friends present in this courtroom (quoting from poetry):

'Step forward, courageous, come to relieve the tired

warrior, not fearing the cross. Grow, flourish, bring forth fruit as Christ's excellent inheritance in the world.'

"I also have a word for you, citizen judges (quoting from poetry):

'And let them by lying articles brand us, not skimping on falsehood. Our path is appointed by Christ, and that means the goal of life is justified.'"

Based on Articles 142-2 and 190-1 of the Criminal Law Code, the Russian Soviet Federal Socialist Republic court sentenced Konshaubi Dzhangetov to three years' deprivation of freedom in strict regime camps and Sergei Dubitsky to three years' deprivation of freedom in ordinary regime camps.

Article 142 reads: "The breaking of the laws of separation of the church from the state and of the school from the church."

Article 190 reads: "The intentional spreading of false fabrications discrediting to the Soviet government and public order."

To learn more about the persecution of Evangelical Baptists in the Soviet Union, write:

Georgi P. Vins
International Representation, Inc.
P.O. Box 1188
Elkhart, Indiana 46515
U.S.A.